IMAGES
of America
OLD KITTERY

By
John D. Bardwell

ARCADIA

First published 1995
Copyright © John D. Bardwell, 1995

ISBN 0-7524-0088-6

Published by Arcadia Publishing,
an imprint of the Chalford Publishing Corporation
One Washington Center, Dover, New Hampshire 03820
Printed in Great Britain

To my uncle, LeRoy S. Fernald, a lifelong resident of Kittery,
a longtime employee of the Navy Yard,
and a member of the Fernald clan

OTHER PUBLICATIONS BY JOHN D. BARDWELL

A Diary of the Portsmouth, Kittery and York Electric Railroad (1986)
A History of the Country Club at York, Maine (1988)
The Isles of Shoals: A Visual History (1989)
A History of York Harbor and the York Harbor Reading Room (1993)
Old York Beach (1994)
Old York (1994)
Ogunquit By-The-Sea (1994)
"Greece: An Archaeological Treasure Chest," from *American Photographs At
the Turn of the Century: Travel and Trekking* (1994)

PUBLICATIONS BY JOHN D. BARDWELL AND RONALD P.
BERGERON

*Images of a University: A Photographic History of the University of New
Hampshire* (1984)
The White Mountains of New Hampshire: A Visual History (1989)
The Lakes Region of New Hampshire: A Visual History (1989)

PUBLICATIONS BY JOHN D. BARDWELL AND PETER A. MOORE

A History of the York Beach Fire Department: 1890–1990 (1990)

Contents

IN MEMORY OF
THE CONTINENTAL SLOOP OF WAR
RANGER
LAUNCHED FROM THIS ISLAND
MAY 10, 1777
SAILED FOR FRANCE NOVEMBER 1,1777
JOHN PAUL JONES, CAPTAIN.
WITH DISPATCHES OF
BURGOYNE'S SURRENDER,
RECEIVED FEBRUARY 14, 1778.
THE FIRST SALUTE
TO THE STARS AND STRIPES
FROM THE FRENCH FLEET
CAPTURED THE
BRITISH SLOOP OF WAR DRAKE
APRIL 24, 1778.

ERECTED BY THE PAUL JONES CLUB
OF PORTSMOUTH
SONS OF THE AMERICAN REVOLUTION
1905

The tablet commemorating the *Ranger* as it appeared in 1905. At that time it was located on Badger's Island where the historic vessel was built.

Introduction

Old Kittery takes its name from the manor of Kittery Court, located on Kittery Point in Kingsweare, in the county of Devon, England. It was from Kingsweare that the Shapleighs came to settle in Kittery Point, Maine. Kingsweare is 10 miles south of the birthplace of another Kittery Point pioneer, Captain Francis Champernowne.

Kittery included 61,457 acres or approximately 96 square miles when it was incorporated in 1647. The separation of Eliot, Berwick, and North Berwick left Kittery with 7,347 acres or approximately 12 square miles. The town also included five islands in the Isle of Shoals group: Appledore, Smuttynose, Cedar, Malaga, and Duck Island were claimed in the Gorges grant and became part of the state of Maine.

Like so many coastal towns in Maine, Kittery was a fishing and shipbuilding community that became involved in the tourist business after the Civil War. Large summer hotels were built on the Isles of Shoals and in Kittery Point and the resort facilities expanded as trains and trolley cars brought increasing numbers of summer visitors to enjoy the beaches and the summer breezes. The eventual increase in automobile traffic led to the growth of roadside services along US Route One, including restaurants, cabins, filling stations, and snack bars.

Shipbuilding brought a flood of defense workers to Kittery during World War II, and maritime history is a vital part of Kittery's heritage. The fisheries have been seriously depleted and the riches of the sea that were discovered by Captain John Smith are no longer productive, but Kittery's characterizing features do continue today, albeit in a different form. Submarines, yachts, lobsters boats, and pleasure boats now share Kittery's waterways and perpetuate the maritime tradition.

The photographs and sketches in this book have been selected to illustrate the unique nature of Kittery's history. They were gathered with the cooperation of Kittery residents who together have made this presentation possible.

John D. Bardwell

The *Ranger*.

One

A Legacy of Shipbuilders

A sail plan of the frigate *Raleigh*. The Continental Congress authorized the construction of thirteen frigates. The *Raleigh* was built on Badger's Island in 1776, and took just six months to complete.

John Paul Jones, one of the most colorful captains in the history of the US Navy, was very much involved in the construction of the *Ranger*, which was commissioned in 1777.

A view of Portsmouth from the Naval Shipyard. The sixteen-gun sloop *Ranger* was built on the same blocks as the *Raleigh*.

The *Ranger* and the *Drake* in battle. The *Ranger* was the first man-of-war to fly the new American flag and the first to receive an official salute from a foreign nation. The new American warship took many prizes between 1778 and 1780.

The *Ranger* in battle.

The *Congress*, a thirty-eight-gun frigate, was built in 1799.

The *Portsmouth*, a twenty-one-gun sloop, was built in 1797.

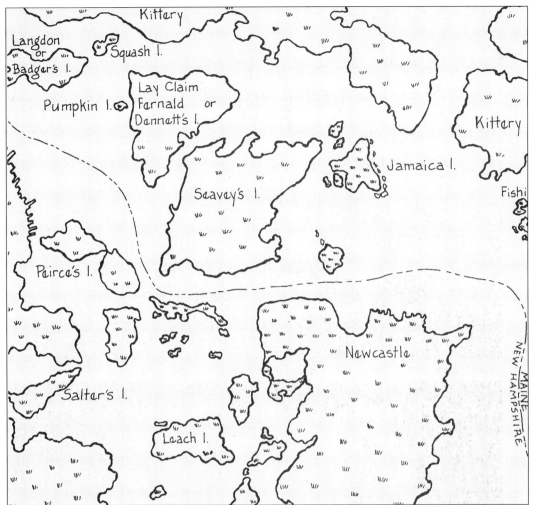

John Fernald, Jr., a shipwright, owned Lay Claim Island, sometimes called Fernald's Island, which had been in the possession of the Fernald family since 1645. He was forced out of business when all of his workers left to build the *Ranger* on nearby Badger's Island. A US Navy report indicated that Fernald's Island "was the best and most suitable place for a dock or building yard and was near to Kittery where all the workers reside." The island was purchased on June 12, 1800, and the first US Naval Shipyard was established there.

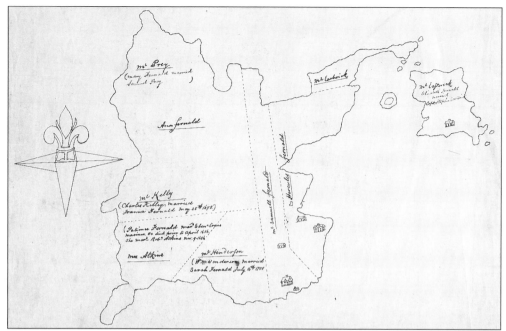

A 1702 map of Fernald's Island. In 1645, Richard Vines, the personal agent of Sir Ferdinando Gorges, rented the islands to Thomas Fernald for an annual fee of two shillings and sixpence.

The *Santee*, a forty-four-gun frigate, was started in 1820 but not finished until 1855. Because it was a sailing ship, it was of little use in the Civil War and it was finally broken up about 1880.

Lieutenant Thomas MacDonough was placed in charge of the new government yard at the beginning of the War of 1812. He was replaced by Commodore Isaac Hull in 1813.

The *Kearsarge*, a steam-screw sailing sloop of war, was built at the Shipyard during the Civil War period. She was propelled by both sail and steam.

The *Kearsarge* engaged the Confederate raider *Alabama* off the coast of Cherbourg, France, in June 1864. The *Alabama* had been at sea for twenty-two months and had destroyed sixty-five Union vessels. Many others had been captured and released under bond.

The *Kearsarge* sank the *Alabama* and ended her destruction of Union shipping. In 1984, French coast guard minesweepers located the wreck of the *Alabama* at a depth of more than 150 feet. After five years of preliminary surveys, nearly two hundred relics were recovered in 1993.

The officers of the *Kearsarge*.

The rescue of the Greely Expedition. Six members of the 1881–1884 Arctic expedition were rescued; twelve others perished.

The rescue team brought relief to the six survivors of the ill-fated expedition in 1884.

Lieutenant A.W. Greely was brought to the Shipyard by the relief vessel that rescued him from the Arctic.

The survivors of the Greely Expedition on August 5, 1884. Lieutenant Greely, standing, remained at the Shipyard to recuperate. He was housed in Quarters R at the naval prison.

Workmen at the Shipyard.

Quarters A and B behind the bandstand in a photograph dating from April 8, 1914.

The USS *Constitution* was towed to the Shipyard, decked over, and used as a receiving ship.

EXPLOSION

HENDERSON POINT

❧

SATURDAY, JULY 22, 1905, 4 P. M.

❧

**ADMIT BEARER TO OBSERVATION GROUNDS,
PIERCE'S ISLAND, MOSES' ISLAND, GOAT ISLAND
OR OLIVER PASTURE IN NEWCASTLE**
(CONNECTED BY PONTOON BRIDGE, FOOT OF GATES ST.)

GEO. H. KEYES

COMPLIMENTARY

This complimentary pass to observe the explosion at Henderson Point permitted the bearer to watch the proceedings from the Portsmouth-New Castle side of the river.

Inside the Henderson Point Coffer Dam that was blown away on July 22, 1905.

22

Henderson Point, on Seavey's Island, extended 500 feet into the Piscataqua River. The point narrowed the channel and forced a swift run of tide which was difficult for the ships to navigate.

The point was blown up after three years of preparation by hundreds of men. The explosion removed 70,000 tons of rock with the detonation of 46 tons of dynamite. The only injury was to a timid citizen who was run over while trying to flee the area.

An aerial view of the Shipyard.

The navy decided to build its first submarine at the Shipyard and the keel of the L-8 was laid in the Franklin shiphouse in late 1914.

The L-8 under construction in April 1916. She was completed in 1917 and was the forerunner of a long line of submarines built at the Shipyard. The facility was officially designated a submarine yard by the secretary of the navy in 1923.

An interior view of the submarine model shed where scale models were built to guide the design and construction of underwater craft.

The O-1 was the second submarine built at the Shipyard. It is shown here in dry dock with workers on the scaffolding.

An S-Boat at Berth One. Eleven S-Boats were launched at the Shipyard between January 1, 1919, and July 14, 1923. This class of submarines was small by later standards.

The S-48 being hauled into the shiphouse for major alterations on February 3, 1927. Three locomotives and two cranes pulled the submarine out in about twenty minutes.

A river view of the S-48 being hauled into the shiphouse. The town of Kittery can be seen in the background.

The S-48 in dry dock.

Locomotive Number Four was one of the three that pulled the S-48 into the shiphouse to be overhauled.

The V-1 (*Barracuda*) on the launching ways on July 16, 1924. She was 341 feet long, cost $7 million to build, and operated at a depth of 200 feet. In 1925, the V-1 traveled 17,000 miles on a cruise for extended trials.

Construction of the pressure hull of the USS *Catchalot* on February 13, 1932. The *Catchalot* was the last of the riveted-hull submarines.

USS *Squalus* sank off the Isles of Shoals on May 23, 1939, while on sea trials. The McCann rescue chamber was rushed from New London, Connecticut, and the first of thirty-three survivors were brought to the surface on the following day.

The *Squalus* was raised on September 13, towed to the Shipyard, rebuilt, and commissioned as the USS *Sailfish* just a year after the sinking.

A diver being lowered into 240 feet of water to aid in the rescue of the *Squalus* survivors.

The bridge and conning tower of the *Sailfish* were placed on the mall at the Shipyard as a memorial to the twenty-six officers and men who were lost on the *Squalus*.

The *Sailfish* returned in the fall of 1945, with a successful war record against Japanese shipping in the Pacific.

A German officer at the surrender of the U-234 on May 19, 1945. After the surrender of Germany, U-boats were towed into the Shipyard and the crews were held at the naval prison until they were transferred to the facilities of the First Army Command.

German submarines were held at the Shipyard for extensive study and German prisoners were required to explain the various systems to naval authorities.

German U-boats U-2513, U-3008, and U-505 berthed at the Shipyard after being surrendered by the Germans. The U-505 was towed to Chicago and installed as a war memorial at the Museum of Science and Industry.

Memorial services for 129 members of the *Thresher* crew were conducted at the *Squalus/Sailfish* memorial on April 15, 1963. The *Thresher* went out for sea trials on April 9, 1963. She made a test dive and never resurfaced.

Christening the *Sand Lance*. Senator Thomas McIntyre was sprayed with champagne when his wife broke the bottle on the bow. At the 1969 event, Senator McIntyre remarked, "This particular launch has a certain sadness to it for this *Sand Lance* may have the dubious distinction of being the last submarine ever built at this yard."

The complete bow of the *Albacore* being lowered into position for installation.

A workman examining a quarter-scale model of the *Albacore* prior to the construction of the experimental submarine.

The *Albacore* (SS569) represented a dramatic advance in submarine design. Built in 1953, it was the fastest and most maneuverable submarine of its time. The hydrodynamic design led to the development of fast attack and nuclear submarines.

The *Albacore* being prepared for the trip to Albacore Park, a submarine museum on the Portsmouth waterfront.

Crew members relaxing in the *Albacore* reading room.

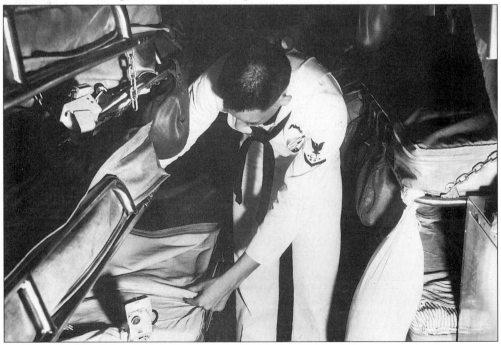

Bunks on the *Albacore*.

"Turning the roast" in the *Albacore* galley.

The Memorial Bridge spans the Piscataqua River between Maine and New Hampshire. The mid-channel of the river is the boundary line between the two states. The bridge was dedicated as a memorial to the soldiers and sailors from Maine and New Hampshire who served in World War I.

Two
Bridging the Piscataqua

The Kittery shoreline from the south abutment site in Portsmouth.

The North Pier caisson. Construction of the Memorial Bridge was begun in 1920 and completed in 1923, at a cost of $1.5 million. It was financed by the US Government and the states of Maine and New Hampshire.

Launching the north caisson on April 21, 1921. Two caissons were filled with fourteen thousand barrels of cement, 6,000 tons of sand, and 12,000 tons of gravel.

Badger's Island on December 11, 1921.

Badger's Island on May 15, 1922. The spans were designed to rest on these concrete shore abutments and the two concrete piers in mid-river.

The first span was in put place on July 8, 1922. The bridge required three spans, each 300 feet in length and weighing 750 tons.

The center span had a vertical lift of 150 feet above the water. The lift was designed to be electrically operated and counterbalanced by concrete weights suspended from cables running over sheaves in the tops of the towers.

The middle span being moved into place on December 28, 1922. Each span was assembled on the shore and floated into position on lighters.

The tomb of Master William Badger who owned the western part of Badger's Island and operated a thriving shipyard where he built nearly one hundred vessels.

Near the site of the old ferry landing in Kittery was the Rice Tavern, which provided creature comforts for travelers and was a stopping point on the stage route. The ferry service ended in 1822 when a new pile bridge to Portsmouth was opened up to traffic.

Three
Old Kittery

This beautiful park at the entrance to Kittery was dedicated on November 11, 1924.

The first Methodist church was dedicated on November 24, 1835.

The first Christian church was about a half mile from Hutchin's Corner on the Haley Road. It was organized in 1806. This building was built and dedicated in 1850, replacing the one that was destroyed by fire in 1849. In an adjoining cemetery is the grave of Elder Mark Fernald, pioneer preacher of the denomination.

The second Methodist Episcopal church was organized in 1866. The building was completed and dedicated on December 31, 1868. The lot was donated by Miss Sarah Ann Elizabeth Rice, one of the last survivors of the Rice family dynasty.

The second Christian church was organized in 1843. The original building burned in 1896 and was replaced the same year. The adjoining parsonage was purchased in 1886.

The Free Will Baptist Church, organized in 1827, stood on the left side of the entrance to the Haley Road. The church building was begun in 1873 and dedicated on December 14, 1875. A guided weathercock was described in the old church records as "the bird."

St. Raphael's Catholic Church.

The Harriet H. Shapleigh School, built in 1912. It was named for a veteran teacher who was also a pioneer suffragist and a descendant of one of Kittery's early settlers.

The Wentworth-Dennett School. This building was completed in 1923 at a cost of $50,000. It was planned to serve the school population of Navy Yard Village and the western sections of town. The grade school had eight rooms and a seating capacity of 322 pupils. It replaced two obsolete buildings, including the last one-room schoolhouse in town.

The Wentworth School in 1912. This school was replaced by the Wentworth-Dennett School when the latter opened in 1923.

The Wentworth School was remodeled for use as a town hall after the pupils were moved to the new building on Rice's Hill.

The Horace Mitchell School, a four-room grade school, was built in 1905. It replaced several one-room schools in this section of town and was named for a public-spirited citizen and hotel man who did much for the town's improvement and welfare.

The Austin School was built in 1875 and named for Reverend Daniel Austin, a retired Unitarian minister who lived in the neighborhood. Daniel Austin donated the bell for the school. Originally a two-room building, it was enlarged to include four rooms in 1919.

A Kittery baseball team. The players are, left to right: (first row) C. Abel, unknown, N. Morrow, K. Pruet, and J. Cutts; (second row) W.S. Spinney, unknown, B. Frisbee, J. Cook, and W. Robbins; (third row) T. Morrow, F. Wilson, W. Wurm, and N. Powell.

A Traip Academy basketball team. The players are, left to right: (first row) Bart Cole, John Morrow, Solon Frisbee, Charles Staples, and John Smart; (back row) Coach Blanchard, Carl Durgin, Dusty Rhodes, and Alex Perry.

Robert W. Traip Academy was built in 1905 at a cost of $40,000, including the cost of the land. It was named for the testator of a fund in the days before free high schools were common in country towns. It became the high school in the town's educational system.

The 1946 Traip Academy basketball team won the Small Schools State Championship by beating Greenville 34 to 25 in Bangor. The players are, left to right: (front row) William Chick, Joseph Pruett, Arthur Willette, Loring Franklin, Richard Milliken, and Lenox Stevens; (back row) Coach Jerald Twitchell, Leon Abbott, Allen Bishop, Charles Knowles, David Remick, Ralph Casella, Elmer Burnham, and Charles Cutten.

The 1946 cross country team remained undefeated for the third consecutive year in regular cross country competition. Here we have, left to right: (front row) Charles Cutten, Harrison Hayford, Kenneth Langton, Lester Clough, and Jack Burnham; (standing) Clifton Trefethen, George Bishop, Charles Welts, William Crawford, and Coach Herbert.

The 1946 girls basketball team. The girls are, left to right: (front row) Louise Small, Gloria Libby, Mildred Strong, Florence Tarling, Diane Jackson, and Beverley Johnston; (middle row) Theresa Dion, Lorraine Guay, Edith Seaward, Ruth Tiano, Eleanor Cressey, Ruth Seaward, and Virginia Lemont; (back row) Josephine Varney, Marilyn Bartlett, Coach Andre La Pointe, Beverley Blanc, and Marguerite DesJardins.

The 1946 Traip football team, undefeated in twenty-two straight games, won the Seaboard League Trophy for the third consecutive year. During this season, they outscored their opponents 204 to 33. The team consisted of, from left to right: (front row) David Remick, Francis Haley, Joseph Pruett, Arthur Willette, Ralph Casella, Charles Knowles, and Albert Smith; (middle row) Charles Mitchell, Robert Tobey, Howard Noyes, George Bishop, Paul Goss, Leon Abbott, and Coach Jack Cannell; (back row) Richard Knudson, Loring Franklin, Dick Milliken, Lenox Stevens, Joseph Florentine, Earl Sanders, and Morris Patch.

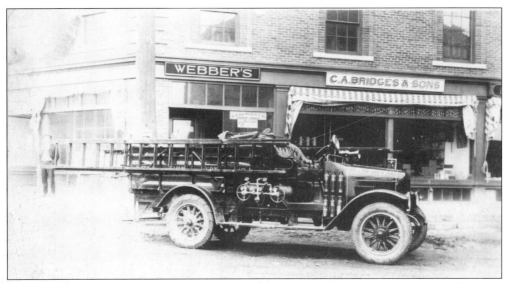

A Kittery fire truck in front of the Fraternal Block. The ground floor of the building was occupied by a bank and other businesses.

A salesman seeking state and county agents to sell the Liberty Motor Firing System. It promised to eliminate ninety percent of all motor troubles. Harold Grace is the man on the left.

Wallingford Square was named in memory of a local boy who made the supreme sacrifice in France during World War I.

The Kittery Fraternal Block was erected in 1923 by the Odd Fellows, the Knights of Pythias, and the Masons, who all used the building. The lot and the building represent an investment of approximately $80,000. There was a spacious hall on the second floor and a dining room and kitchen for banquets and suppers in the basement.

Grace's Auto Service building undergoing repairs in 1946.

Construction of the interstate highway overpass at Dennett Road. Durgin's bus garage at James Corner can be seen in the background.

Hubs Service Station in Wallingford Square was operated by Steve Foley.

Kittery Laundry and the Ranger bowling alleys.

The interior of Kittery Laundry.

The employees of Kittery Laundry pose with the laundry trucks.

Kittery Laundry delivery trucks lined up for a group picture.

An early postcard view of Rodgers Road.

The entrance to the Shipyard at Wallingford Square. Visitors were welcome but the guard at the gate inquired about the nature of your business. A special pass was required to enter the workshops and use cameras. Note the house at left which has since been turned to face the main street.

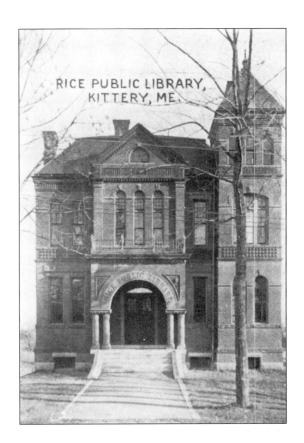

The Rice Public Library. This institution was endowed by Miss Arabella Rice of Boston and Portsmouth, in memory of her father, Robert Rice, who was a native of Kittery.

The road to Badger's Island from Kittery in the early 1900s.

The Hotel Champernowne at Kittery Point was built by Horace Mitchell in 1890. He used his influence to route the Portsmouth, Kittery, and York trolley line through Kittery Point and thus provide convenient transportation to the hotels in the area.

The Hotel Champernowne during the 1912 season. The hotel was taken over by the US Navy during World War I and used to house officers and men.

Four

Kittery Point

A lobster shack at Kittery Point.

The Pepperrell house was built by Edward F. Safford in 1872 and enlarged in 1885. Later, he added four cottages.

The Hotel Park Field in 1920. Erected in 1887 for Jesse E. Frisbee, it was named for a deer park that existed here in the days of Sir William Pepperrell. It was later called the Piscataqua Inn.

Fort McClary, originally Fort William, was located on a 30-acre site in Kittery Point. The old blockhouse, built in 1842, is surrounded by the unfinished granite work of the Civil War period. The fort was renamed to honor Major Andrew McClary who fought with General Stark's regiment at Bunker Hill.

The Kittery Point Post Office is the building on the left of this photograph. In 1953, it was painted gray with a bright red door.

The tomb of the Pepperrell family is just across the road from the old Pepperrell mansion.

LT. GEN. SIR WM. PEPPERRELL, Bart.
The Victor of Louisbourg A.D. 1745.

Sir William Pepperrell commanded English regiments at the capture of Louisbourg in 1745. For this service, he was created a baronet by King George II on November 15, 1746. Pepperrell inherited his father's home in Kittery Point which he expanded and redecorated.

The Sparhawk Hall, built in 1742, was originally the residence of Colonel Nathaniel Sparhawk, son-in-law of Sir William Pepperrell. It was later occupied by the Saffords, the Dearings, the Penhallows, the Browns, and the Honorable Horace Mitchell.

The hallway at Sparhawk Hall. From the broad hallway with its paneled wainscotting the stairs, with their elaborately carved balusters, sweep gracefully to a broad landing crowned by a Palladian window.

The residence of Sir William Pepperrell, the leading New England American of the Colonial period. He was known for his business ability and integrity, and as an executive, a gentleman, and a colonizer.

Between 1725 and 1775 the old Pepperrell mansion was one of the great houses of Colonial America. The estate stretched for 30 miles along the Maine coast. Pepperrell's home at Kittery Point was based on the English way of life—fully paneled walls, many portraits, liveried servants, a deer park, and beautiful gardens.

The drawing room at the Pepperrell mansion. The distinguishing feature of a mansion in Colonial times appears to have been the quality of the woodwork and furnishings. The Pepperrell mansion, despite the early date of the building, possessed magnificent interiors with woodwork that has never been excelled.

The old Bray house, built *c.* 1662, was the home of Marjory Bray, the mother of Sir William Pepperrell.

The drawing room at the Bray house. This is considered to be one of the oldest dwelling houses in Maine and it has served as a tavern, a seat of the local court, and possibly as a private school.

The Pelatiah Fernald House was built in 1798 by Captain John Moore and sold to Pelatiah Fernald, a sea captain. It stood across the street from the home of Pelatiah's brother, the preacher Elder Mark Fernald. In 1897, it was sold to George S. Wasson, artist and writer.

The Whipple House was the birthplace of General William Whipple, one of the signers of the Declaration of Independence. It was built on the southeastern margin of Locke's Cove, originally called Whipple's Cove.

The summer residence of William Dean Howells, dean of American letters. It was here that Mark Twain, Hamlin Carland, and other noted authors visited with Mr. Howells.

The Lady Pepperrell house. Lady Pepperrell built this house in 1765 after her husband died. She was fifty-seven years old at the time. She loved her church and may have built her home in this location lest old age should make it difficult for her to attend services.

The old Congregational parsonage was built in 1729 and is probably the oldest parsonage in Maine, if not the oldest in New England.

The Robert F. Gerrish house is approached by a lane that winds past the parish burying ground. One end of the house was probably built as early as 1700, the other end being added several years later. Much of this house is wainscotted and it has sliding window shutters.

The Thaxter home on Cutts Island. Built on the site of one of the homes of Captain Francis Champernowne, the property was acquired by John and Roland Thaxter in 1880. The sons of Celia Thaxter razed the old building and incorporated many of the old timbers in a house that later became the residence of Miss Rosamond Thaxter and her mother, Mrs. Mary Gertrude Stoddard Thaxter.

The cairn of Captain Francis Champernowne on Cutts Island. Champernowne, a nephew of Sir Ferdinando Gorges, married the widow of Robert Cutts of Kittery. He owned three houses, two of which were on Cutts Island.

Kittery Point Bridge.

Chauncey Creek separates Gerrish Island from the mainland.

The *Gracie* G., a deep sea fishing boat that sailed out of Kittery Point on Sundays and holidays. The fee was $2 including the bait and lines. The vessel could accommodate up to eighty passengers.

Local fishermen Horace Mitchell and friend holding a large codfish for the photographer.

The old West Indies Store at Pepperrell Cove.

The old pier at Pepperrell Cove.

Pepperrell Cove water skiers in action. They are, from left to right, Barbara Carlson, Linda Parsons, and Ann Grace.

Members of the Pepperrell Cove Water Ski Club.

Artist Russell Cheney and young Frank Frisbee.

Trefethen's Wharf.

George Smart, Kittery police chief.

A Kittery Point fire truck.

Safford School, named for Elder Moses Safford, was built as a district school in 1871/72.

A festive gathering featuring flags and a tent, jury-rigged, to provide shade for the celebrants.

Edna in her white graduation dress at the corner of the piazza.

A Kittery shoreline.

A steamboat on the river. Steamboats provided transportation along the coast and to the Isles of Shoals.

Five
Tourist Services

Greenmoors Inn on Route One between Kittery and York. It later became the Stardust nightclub and a Chinese restaurant before being incorporated into the Kittery Outlet Mall complex.

The Maine Information Center was a prominent building on Route One in Kittery. It was a comfort station and publicity bureau for travelers along this route.

Ripley's Inn and Cabins. The cabins had electric lights, linoleum-covered floors, Simmons beds, hot and cold water, showers, toilets, lavatories, and stoves.

Ripley's was your home away from home. It featured good food, properly cooked. The facilities were located on Route One, 2 miles east of Portsmouth.

Westwold Motor Court. Route One in Kittery was once the gateway to Maine and travel services began to line the highway as auto traffic increased.

Gunnison's gas station.

Durgin Park provided a wide range of services for the traveler. There was food service for the people and fuel service for the vehicles.

The Durgin Park complex was isolated when a sweeping curve in the road was straightened and most travelers no longer drove past the facility.

Bing Adams, founder of the Kittery Trading Post. Quoddy moccasins were one of his featured products in the early days.

An early picture of the Kittery Trading Post.

Six
Trains and Trolleys

Portsmouth, Kittery, and York Street Railway car number four passing through Wallingford Square in downtown Kittery.

George Wood, purser on the ferry of the P. K. & Y. trolley (which later became the Atlantic Shore Railway) between Portsmouth and Badger's Island. Woodward had also been a motorman on the trolley to York Beach, *c.* 1915.

The P. K. & Y. ferry crossing the Piscataqua River.

The P. K. & Y. ferry the *Kittery* at Badger's Island.

The ferry landing on Badger's Island.

The *Kittery* approaching the ferry landing in Portsmouth, *c.* 1905.

The Badger's Island ferry landing.

Passengers leaving the ferry for the trolley station.

At right is George Woodward, purser on the ferry, posing at the landing on Badger's Island.

Two trolley operators and one passenger, photographed at the trolley station.

Main St., Kittery, Me.

A postcard view looking down Main Street toward Wallingford Square. Note the trolley tracks leading into the square.

The trolley tracks on the left help us to date this picture of a Kittery street, as we know that the trolley system operated between 1897 and 1923.

The interior of a trolley car with three distinguished-looking passengers carefully posed for the photographer.

P. K. & Y. car number six crossing the Locke's Cove trestle near the present location of Shipyard gate number 2.

The trolley car barn at Kittery Point.

A postcard view of the trolley crossing the trestle at Locke's Cove.

The Kittery Point car barn and power plant, built in 1897 for the P. K. & Y. Street Railway.

Workmen at the P. K. & Y. power plant behind the car barn.

P. K. & Y. car number four near the intersection of Chauncey Creek and Tenny Hill Roads in 1897.

A trolley crossing New Call's trestle at Sea Point.

A work crew at the trolley car barn.

The Kittery Junction depot. The depot was the junction of the Boston & Maine and the York Harbor & Beach Railroads. This postcard was mailed on July 23, 1906.

The Spruce Creek trestle of the York Harbor & Beach Railroad.

The Bedell railroad stop at Kittery Point.

The Kittery Point Railroad Station.

Kittery Junction on August 16, 1894.

Sea Point Beach.

Cookson's Store at Sea Point Beach.

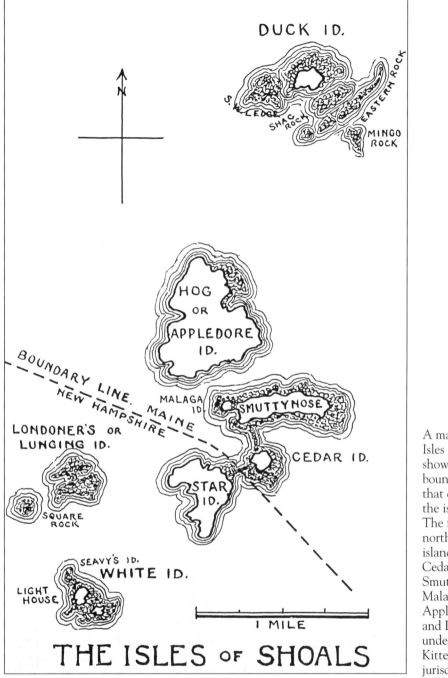

DUCK ID.

S.W. LEDGE

SHAG ROCK

EASTERN ROCK

MINGO ROCK

HOG OR APPLEDORE ID.

BOUNDARY LINE. MAINE

NEW HAMPSHIRE

MALAGA ID.

SMUTTYNOSE

CEDAR ID.

LONDONER'S OR LUNGING ID.

SQUARE ROCK

STAR ID.

SEAVY'S ID. WHITE ID.

LIGHT HOUSE

1 MILE

THE ISLES OF SHOALS

A map of the Isles of Shoals showing the boundary line that divides the islands. The five northern islands, Cedar, Smuttynose, Malaga, Appledore, and Duck, are under Kittery's jurisdiction.

Seven

The Isles of Shoals

The Thaxter house on Cutts Island as it appeared in 1882. Levi Lincoln Thaxter is seated on the lawn.

Whaleboats provided transportation between the islands and offered recreational opportunities for hotel guests. They were also used by local fishermen.

Sailboats at anchor in front of the Appledore House. In 1874, the Laightons built a landing pier on Appledore Island and acquired a small fleet of pleasure boats for their guests.

The Appledore dock being floated into place.

The Appledore dock in 1901.

Rafting in the Appledore tidal pool in 1898. Rafting was a favorite pastime of the young people who vacationed on the island.

Sailing in the tidal pool in 1901. Many young Shoalers had their first sailing lessons in the tidal pool near the Appledore House.

A steamship at the Appledore Pier in 1901. The Laightons did not build a dock until John Poor opened the Oceanic Hotel on Star Island in 1873. Poor built a boat landing for his guests arriving by steamship—a great convenience.

Out for a morning row in 1900. Two senior residents enjoy a trip around the cove.

Making social calls on Appledore Island in 1901. Summer residents dressed for tea and made formal social calls even though they were on a rocky island off the coast of Maine.

Six little rascals model what the well-dressed Shoaler was wearing at the turn of the century.

Colonel Fuller engaging in his favorite pastime. Relaxing on the porch of the Appledore House was an accepted practice at the turn of the century.

A group of veteran Shoalers on the rocks in front of the Appledore House. The ladies kept their hands busy even during periods of relaxation.

Storing the boats at the end of the summer season. It required horsepower and manpower to pull the boats from the water and store them under the hotel porch.

The tidal pool was deserted. A few boats were left on the shore to provide transportation for the people who wintered on the island.

Laying the cable between Star and Appledore to improve communication between the two islands.

The Appledore House opened for business on June 15, 1848. Thomas Laighton moved his family to the island and they helped him operate the hotel which was to attract some of the most accomplished writers, artists, and musicians of its time. It was in the parlor here that Celia Laighton and Levi Thaxter were married.

John Haley Bellamy (1824–1914). Bellamy, a master carver, worked at the Shipyard most of his life.

Eight

People, Places and Things

The Joseph Mitchell Garrison, located at the head of Brave Boat Harbor Creek near the York town line, was probably built on the site of an earlier fort. The one-story building had two rooms without a hallway and a garret reached by ladder. It had a massive center chimney.

The Kittery Fire Department. These men are, left to right: (seated) unknown, Russell Brackett, Waldo "Pete" Staples, "Skinny" Flynn, Chief Oscar Farrington, Raymond Brackett, Ed Littlefield, Howard Keene, and Roger Milliken; (standing, center) unknown, Frank Rhodes, unknown, Roy Fernald, Jed Staples, unknown, Harold Thompson, Gene Hayes, unknown, and Charlie Pratt; (standing in back) H.P. Grace, Ogden Bridges, Wesley Rodgers, Jesse Philbrick, and Henry Fuller.

John Haley Bellamy carved the case for this Masonic shelf clock. (Photograph courtesy of the Scottish Rite Masonic Museum of Our National Heritage)

Another Bellamy work, this typical "eagle with the banner" wall decoration is now housed at the Kittery Historical and Naval Museum.

Bellamy carved this eagle figurehead for the USS *Lancaster* in 1875.

Acknowledgments

I would like to thank the Kittery Historical and Naval Museum, the Portsmouth Naval Shipyard, the Portsmouth Athenaeum, the Portsmouth Masonic Museum, the Star Island Corporation, the Museum of Our National Heritage, the Robert W. Traip Academy, Alice Freeman, Peter Moore, Howard Moulton, Raymond Tobey, O.R. Cummings, James Dolph, John Hutchinson, and Glenn B. Skillin.

Special thanks to Mr. and Mrs. Harold Grace, who generously shared their extensive collection of postcards and photographs as well as their knowledge of Kittery history.

Key To Map of Kittery (on p. 2)

1. Interstate Memorial Bridge; 2. *Ranger* Tablet, Badger's Island; 3. Grave of Master William Badger, Badger's Island; 4. Old Ferry Landing and Rice Tavern; 5. Wentworth-Dennett School; 6. Second Methodist Church (grave of Reverend John Newmarch; 7. Second Christian Church; 8. Site of former Universalist Church; 9. The Doctor Jones House; 10. Wallingford Square (entrance to Naval Shipyard); 11. Home of late General Mark F. Wentworth; 12. Rice Public Library; 13. St. Raphael's Catholic Church; 14. R.W. Traip Academy; 15. Birthplace of General William Whipple; 16. Site of home of Elder William Screven; 17. Austin School; 18. Sparhawk Hall; 19. First Parish Congregational Church and Old Parsonage; 20. Old Congregational Cemetery; 21. Lady Pepperrell House; 22. Old Gerrish House; 23. Summer home of the late William Dean Howells; 24. Fort McClary; 25. Site of the home of Andrew Pepperrell; 26. Pepperrell Mansion and Tomb; 27. Old Bray House; 28. Fomer home of George S. Wasson; 29. Horace Mitchell School; 30. Free Baptist Church and Cemetery; 31. Grave of Elder Moses Safford, Hoyt's Island; 32. First Christian Church; 33. Site of the home of Charles Chauncy; 34. Home of John Thaxter, son of Celia Thaxter; 35. Graves of Captain Francis Champernowne and Mary Chauncy; 36. Eagle Point, Spruce Creek; 37. First Methodist Church; 38. Home and grave of Harriet H. Shapleigh; 39. Shapleigh School; 40. The Isles of Shoals.